Exploring the World of Plants

Exploring the World of Plants

by Penny Raife Durant
Illustrated by Nancy Woodman

A *Try This* Book
Franklin Watts
New York ❧ Chicago ❧ London ❧ Toronto ❧ Sydney

*To my brother, David, and his wife, Ann,
with love.*

Cover illustration copyright ©: Nancy Woodman

Photographs copyright ©:
Visuals Unlimited: pp. 7, 43 (both CABISCO), 11 (SIU), 20, 25 (both D. Newman),
29 (Triarch), 38 (John Trager); Comstock, Inc./Mike and Carol Werner: p 8;
Photo Researchers, Inc.: pp. 10 (Tony Craddock /SPL), 17 (Gregory K. Scott),
18 (Lynwood Chace), 30 (E.R. Degginger), 39 (Nardin/Jacana); Kjell B. Sandved: p. 36;
North Wind Picture Archives: p.44

Library of Congress Cataloging-in-Publication Data

Durant, Penny Raife.
Exploring the world of plants / by Penny Raife Durant.
p. cm. — (Try this series)
Includes index.
ISBN 0-531-20126-0 (lib. bdg.) — ISBN 0-531-15746-6
1. Plants—Juvenile literature. 2. Botany—Juvenile literature.
3. Plants—Experiments—Juvenile literature. 4. Botany—
Experiments—Juvenile literature. [1. Plants—Experiments.
2. Botany—Experiments. 3. Experiments.] I. Title II. Series.
QK49.D87 1995

581—dc20

94-46474
CIP AC

CONTENTS

1

THE WORLD OF PLANTS

Can you imagine a world without plants? Think about the moon or Mars. No plants grow there. Nothing lives there. Without plants, there is no animal life.

Animals of all kinds, including humans, depend on plants. Even animals that eat only other animals depend on plants. A lion may eat a zebra or a wildebeest, but that zebra or wildebeest eats plants.

We depend on plants for many other things as well as food. Plants provide shelter for animals. They provide

These tiny plants, called diatoms, have only one cell. Normally, we cannot see them. They are magnified here 100 times.

us with many products we use every day. The paper to make this book came from a plant. So did the fabric for your jeans. Even your toothpaste probably contains kelp, a kind of seaweed.

Plants come in all sizes. *Diatoms* are plants with just one cell. (To learn how to pronounce any word in *italics* look in the glossary in the back of the book.) They are so small you have to use a microscope to see one. *Sequoias* are huge trees, larger than just about any other living thing. Plants come in all shapes and colors.

Sequoias are one of the largest plants in the world.

Plants are different from animals in many ways. They can't move around looking for food. What they need has to be where they grow.

Plants use carbon dioxide, a gas in the air, to make food. The process is called *photosynthesis*. During photosynthesis, the plant gives off oxygen gas. People and animals breathe in oxygen and breathe out carbon dioxide. Plants turn carbon dioxide into oxygen for us to breathe. We turn the oxygen back into carbon dioxide for the plants to use. This is a wonderful relationship.

The more you know about plants, the more you may want to work with them. *Botanists* are scientists who work with plants. When you do experiments with plants, you can be a botanist, too.

This book will show you many fun ways to experiment with plants. You need some basic supplies such as seeds and soil. But more important, you must have curiosity and be able to observe. Be a botanist and try these activities!

2

SEEDS

Let's observe some seeds. Where will we find them? Seeds can be found in many places, both outdoors and indoors. You may find some in your kitchen.

We eat many types of seeds, such as sunflower seeds, sesame seeds, peas, beans, peanuts, and corn. You will also find seeds in other plants we eat, such as apples, melons, pears, tomatoes, peaches, and other fruits.

There are many different kinds of seeds. Some of the seeds we eat are oats, wheat, sunflower seeds, beans, peanuts, and almonds.

Outdoors you can find seeds anywhere you see plants growing. In some cities, there aren't many yards. But you'll find plants between the cracks in the sidewalk, in planter boxes outside buildings, and in parks. If you live in more open country, you'll find many seeds in your yard, in open fields, and around your town.

Try this: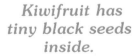

Make a seed-collecting wristband. Take a piece of masking tape and put it around your wrist with the sticky side out. Use wide tape or stick two pieces together side by side. Now go on a seed hunt. Start outside. Look at the ground under flowers and bushes. Look for grass that has grown very long and has seeds on the top. Look for pine cones with seeds protected by spiky scales. Put the seeds you find on your wristband. Look around your kitchen for seeds. Ask if you can cut up fruit to find the seeds. Can you find the seeds of a strawberry?

Kiwifruit has tiny black seeds inside.

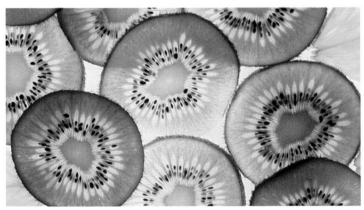

Find as many seeds as you can. Put them all on the wristband. Then cut the tape and take the wristband from your arm. Stretch it out flat. Using a magnifying glass, look at the seeds. Are they all the same? How are they different? Can you remember which seeds came from which plants? Start a plants notebook. Make a list in your notebook of all the seeds you found. Name them if you can. If you don't know the plant name, write down where you found the seed and draw a picture of the plant it came from.

What is the largest seed you found? What is the smallest? Which has the most unusual shape? How many colors of seeds did you find? Are some seeds hard? Save all your seeds. You will use them later.

Parts of Seeds

Seeds come in all sizes and shapes. If you explored your spice shelf for seeds, you might have found poppy or mustard seeds. They are very small. A coconut is a seed, too. It's very large.

Seeds are the beginning of plants. Within some seeds you can observe the beginnings of the different parts of a plant.

Try this:

Add 25 drops of food coloring to half a cup of water. Soak some lima beans or pinto beans overnight in this dyed water. The next day, use your magnifying glass on the beans. Observe the changes in the outside of the seeds. What happened? Let the seeds soak two more days. Then split open a few seeds with your thumbnail. Can you locate all the parts of the seed

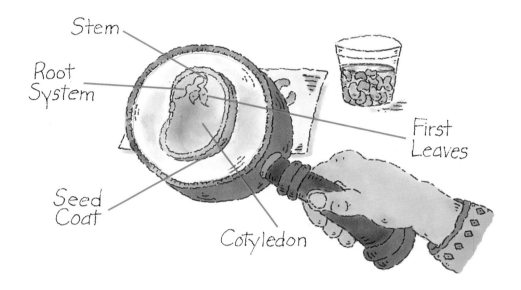

pointed out in the drawing? Can you tell where the water entered the seed? What would happen if you covered that part with a drop of wax from a birthday candle? Try it on a new bean seed and then soak it in dyed water. What happens?

Germination

When a seed begins to change and the beginnings of the new plant emerge, we say it is *germinating*. This is an important part of growing plants.

Ask for an old pair of socks. Put them on over your shoes when you take a walk in a wooded area or open field. Walk through as many types of brush, weeds, and grass as you can. Take off the socks. When you get

home, save one sock in a plastic bag. (You can use the seeds on it for other activities). Plant the other sock in a mixture of potting soil and vermiculite. These are materials sold at gardening supply stores for growing plants. Keep the soil moist and watch to see what might germinate.

Gardeners buy seeds from nurseries, garden centers, and seed companies. The seeds come in packages that can tell you a lot about the seeds. Often the package will tell you when to plant the seeds, where to plant them in your garden, what type of soil is best, and how deep to plant them. Why are these facts important?

Some seeds sprout very fast. Others take a long time to germinate. You need to know this when you experiment with seeds. Some of the fast ones are radishes, marigolds, leaf lettuce, carrots, peas, and beans.

Try this:

First germinate some radish seeds in potting soil. Then try germinating some on a sponge. In sand. On a crumpled tissue. In sawdust. In coffee grounds. What happens? If you keep them moist, will they continue to grow past germination? What have you learned about germinating seeds? What do they need? Make notes in your notebook. What was the most successful *potting medium*?

Did you know that seeds and plants are powerful? Have you ever seen a sidewalk cracked and lifted by tree roots?

Try this:

Take a small plastic bottle with a cork stopper. Fill the bottle with as many pea or bean seeds as will fit.

Add water, enough to cover the seeds. Put the cork stopper on the bottle. Leave it for several days. What happens?

How Seeds Spread

Seeds often fall right beneath the plant from which they came. On your sock, you probably found seeds that came from a plant you didn't see. Sometimes you will find seeds quite a distance from their plants.

The part of the plant surrounding the seed is called the fruit. We eat some fruits, like apples and peaches. Some fruits, like acorns and pine cones, are not edible for humans.

Does the size of the fruit have anything to do with the number of seeds inside it? Compare several fruits, including poppies, peaches, avocados, kiwifruit, tomatoes, and apples.

Each fruit in its own way helps the seeds travel far. This makes it possible for the plant to grow in many new places. People send fruit all over the world because it tastes so good. They eat the fruit, but usually throw away the seeds. The seeds often fall on the ground and germinate. Some small animals bury as many seeds as they can find. Not all of them are eaten. Some grow into new plants. Birds eat fruit and seeds, too. Sometimes they eat the outside of a berry and drop the seed from their mouths while they're flying. So they help the seeds travel, too.

When birds eat berries, they help plants spread by taking the seeds inside to new planting grounds.

Even when animals eat seeds, the seeds are not always digested. The animal droppings contain the seeds. They are still able to grow. A new plant can germinate many miles from where the original plant lives. What kinds of plants do you find growing near your birdbath? Under a fence along the road? Did they grow from seeds dropped by the birds?

Fruits that are not edible have other ways of getting around. Some fruits, such as the fuzz surrounding a thistle seed, are carried on a breeze. The fruit is lightweight. The breeze carries it for a short distance

Dandelion seeds are spread by the wind.

before it drifts to the ground. Other fruits are like helicopters and spin away in the wind. Maple trees give off fruits that act like helicopters.

Some fruits are like saltshakers. During a breeze, the poppy shakes out its seed from a dried fruit after the flower has bloomed. These seeds travel only a few feet or yards, depending on the strength of the wind. Other fruits have burrs that stick to animal fur or people's socks. They can hitchhike long distances.

Some seeds leave their fruit through an explosion. Touch-me-not (or jewelweed) seeds burst from the pod and travel a few feet to a few yards. Others, like the coconut, can float on water. A coconut seed could float from one island to another and then germinate.

Try this:

Gather a cup of seeds of all shapes, sizes, and weights. Outside on the sidewalk, or inside where you

have a large, uninterrupted space, place an electric fan. Turn the fan on low and slowly sift the seeds through your fingers a few inches in front of the fan. Which seeds blow the farthest? What is their shape? Are they heavy or light? Which blow the shortest distance? Use a measuring tape and make a chart in your notebook of the distances several seeds are blown.

3

WHAT PLANTS NEED

Once your seeds germinate, they grow into seedlings. Seedlings are very small, very young plants. Handle seedlings carefully, because they are delicate.

Why are these sunflowers facing the same direction?

Plants grow at different rates. Some, like cacti and many trees, are slow growing. Others are fast growers, like radishes. When you plant seeds in your garden, you often get fast-growing plants that you didn't plant. We call them weeds. But what are weeds? Weeds are plants that live naturally in the soil in our yard—our local soil.

Another name for weeds is *local plants*. Seeds from these plants are usually very quick to sprout and very easy to grow. Look around your yard or neighborhood for some local plants and their seeds. Maybe you have some on your wristband or on the sock you've been saving.

Try this:

Punch small holes in the bottom of four paper cups with a sharp pencil or ballpoint pen. Take four kinds of seeds. Some good seeds to try are lima or pinto beans, corn, pumpkin, pea, radish, or local seeds. Plant them, one type in each of the cups, and put the cups on a tray or plate. Label each cup with the type of seed. Add a little water to each cup. Keep the soil moist and make sure the plants get plenty of sunlight.

Make a chart to record the growth of each sprout. Measure them in three days, five days, one week, and two weeks. Measure the height of the plant from seed to tip. Count the number of leaves. Measure the width at the widest part. Note any bud development. Record all this information in your notebook.

Before your seeds germinate, try to guess which will grow the fastest. Scientists often make a guess, called a *hypothesis*. Then they test the hypothesis to find out if they were right or wrong. Don't worry if you were wrong. You'll learn from the experiment either way.

The plants will grow if you provide them with what they need. What do plants need to grow? See if you can list several things.

Light

Photosynthesis means making things with light. Plants need light to grow. *Chlorophyll*, the substance that makes plants green, absorbs the light. The plant takes in carbon dioxide from the air. With the help of light and water, the plant returns oxygen to the air and grows leaves, stems, and other plant parts.

Try this:

Plant grass seed in a shallow pan of potting soil. Keep the soil moist and in a warm, sunny spot. Wait until the grass is half an inch long (about a centimeter). Then place a small box over some grass at one end. Place a clean jar over some grass at the other end. Leave the box and jar in place for a week. At the end of the week, remove the box and jar. What happened?

Light and heat from the sun came into the jar, but the glass did not allow the heat to be reflected back out of the jar. The jar made a greenhouse for the grass. Greenhouses help plants grow by trapping heat inside. The box blocked the light from the grass. Do plants need light? Will more light mean more growth?

Try this:

Take two plants the same size, and with the same number of leaves. Set them both in a sunny place. Water them when they need it. Make a *reflector* with aluminum foil around the bottom of only one plant. Watch the plants for about three weeks. Count the

leaves again. Observe all the leaves carefully. Measure the plants. Did the reflector make a difference?

Plants need light to grow, but what can a plant do if it is not getting enough light? What happens when you leave a houseplant along a window sill for a week? Look at the stems and leaves. Which way are they facing? Turn the plant around 180 degrees. Look at the stems and leaves in another week.

The leaves turn toward the light. That's because the plant cells on the side away from the light grow longer. The cells facing the light don't change, so the stems bend toward the light.

Plants, like these bean sprouts, can bend toward the light.

Try this:

Germinate a bean seed in a paper cup filled with damp soil. Make a maze in a shoe box with three pieces of cardboard and tape, as shown in the drawing. Make a hole in the box at one end. Place the cup with the bean sprout at the other end and close the box. Put the box near a lamp so that light shines in the hole. Leave it for several days. Then open the maze and see what happened.

Phototropism is the movement of plants toward the light. Look for signs of phototropism in your houseplants or plants against a wall or fence.

Water

When you plant something, you must water it. Already, you have been watering plants and keeping seedlings moist. You know that plants need water for the process of photosynthesis. What happens if a plant does not get enough water?

Cut a stalk of celery, with or without leaves. Leave it unwrapped in the refrigerator, where the air is dry. After a few days, pick up the celery by its large end. Try to hold it upright. Does the top bend? The celery is wilting because the air has absorbed water from the celery.

If the celery has not wilted too much (the top should bend only slightly), cut about half an inch off the bottom of the celery. Water can then enter the cells at that end of the celery. Put the celery in a glass of water for several hours. What happens now when you press the top?

How does the water in the glass help the celery cells? *Turgor pressure* is the pressure of water in the cells of a plant. Without enough turgor pressure, the plant wilts and eventually dies.

Try this:

Take three cups of water. Put one-fourth cup of sugar in one cup. Stir well. Put eight to ten drops of food coloring in another cup of water. Leave the third plain. Label the cups with "sugar," "color," and "plain." Cut three stalks of celery with leaves at the top. Put one, bottom first, in each cup of water. Watch it occasionally for two days. What happens? Taste the leaves of the celery in sugar water.

Water can actually move through the walls of plant cells by a process called *osmosis.* And any substance dissolved in the water moves with the water from cell to cell in the plant.

We know that plants take in water, but do they use it all?

Try this:

Tie a plastic bag over several leaves growing on a houseplant. Leave the plant in the sunlight for two or three hours. Look closely at the bag. What happened?

Water evaporated out of openings in the leaves

called *stomates*. This process is called *transpiration*. When the water evaporated, it entered the air in the plastic bag. A plant transpires about 90 percent of the water it takes in. Remember to take off the plastic bag when you have finished this activity.

Where are the stomates of a leaf located? Look at the underside of the leaves of a wandering Jew plant. The stomates are bright green. Can you find the stomates on other leaves?

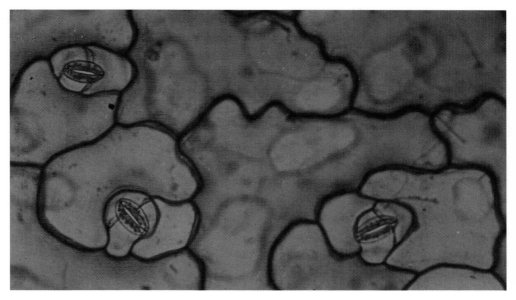

This leaf has been magnified and dyed to show stomates, tiny openings within cells. Stomates allow water to evaporate from plants.

Some plants live in water. They are called *aquatic* plants. Water lilies are one type of aquatic plant. However, too much water can be bad for some plants,

The water lily is an aquatic plant.
Its leaves and flowers float on top of ponds.

especially beans and peas. The roots and seeds can rot if they are overwatered. It is important for plants to have water available, but not too much. That is why you should punch holes in the bottom of cups you plant seeds in. If there is too much water, it can run out through the holes.

Food from the Soil

Most plants require water, light, and soil. Some can live just in water, but most thrive only in soil that contains the food, the *nutrients*, they need. When you broke apart the bean seed, you saw that the seed had a part called a *cotyledon*. The cotyledon contains energy and nutrition for the emerging plant. After the seed sprouted and the bean plant began to grow, what happened to the cotyledon?

Place four bean seeds between moist paper towels and the inside walls of a jar. Using a thin, permanent black marker on the outside of the glass, trace around the shape of the bean. Add a small amount of water to the jar. Put the jar in a sunny spot. Check it every day and

keep the paper towels moist. After one week, trace the cotyledons with a thin red marker on the outside of the jar. After three weeks, trace them again with a green marker. What happens to the cotyledons?

Now soak some more beans for several days. When you open them, carefully remove the small plant. Put the beans on top of a cup filled with potting soil. Keep them moist. Will they grow without the cotyledons?

The seed gets its nutrients from the cotyledon until roots can grow. Then the roots absorb nutrients from water and soil.

Topsoil is the uppermost, fertile layer of soil in your garden. It contains minerals, which are plant nutrients, and *humus*. Humus is dead plant material. It has many nutrients that plants need. Soil usually also contains water and air.

Try this:

Take a clear glass jar. Fill it one-third full with topsoil from your garden or school yard. Add water and put the lid on. Then shake it well. Let the mixture settle for a few days. Don't move it at all. What happens? Use a magnifying glass to look at any layers that formed. Can you name the different parts of your soil? Do you find sand, clay, humus? Try this activity with soil from deeper down and from other locations. How are they different?

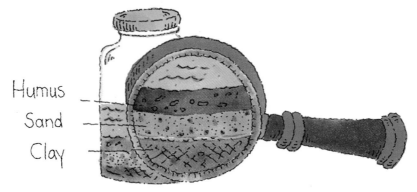

Humus
Sand
Clay

Not every area of the earth has the same amount of topsoil. There may be as little as one-fourth of an inch of topsoil in mountainous areas. In areas where a lot of farming is done, there may be as much as 6 feet (2 m)!

Wind and rain can take away, or *erode*, topsoil. It can also erode when too many animals eat the grass of an area or when people build things there. The more topsoil, the better plants can grow. The amount of topsoil helps determine the types of plants that grow in different parts of the world.

Try this:

Collect five different types of soil in jars: potting soil, garden soil, peat moss, sand, and clay. You may have to hunt a bit to find them. Put each type of soil in a paper cup with holes punched in the bottom. Set the cups on a tray. Try germinating seeds in each type. Keep a

record of how quickly they germinated, the number and size of their leaves, and the condition of the plants at different stages of their growth. Which soil is best for your seeds?

It is also important that plants have enough room to grow. If you have ever walked through a dense pine forest, you probably noticed how skinny the trees were. When trees are close together, they have to grow tall quickly to reach the sunlight. Where they have more room, they can grow outward and upward. Their trunks are thicker. Their branches are lower and spread out in a larger circle.

Gravity

We have seen that plant growth depends on several things. Most plants must have light, water, and soil to grow. What else makes a difference in plant growth?

Try this: 〜〜〜〜〜〜〜〜〜〜〜〜〜〜〜〜〜

Put some bean seeds into a jar with damp cotton balls. After the stems are as tall as the jar, turn the jar on its side. Keep the cotton moist as the seedlings grow. Be careful not to overwater them. What happens to the stems? Which way do they turn?

Gravity affects plant growth. It tells roots to grow down and stems to grow up.

Try this:

Germinate some bean seeds in a jar with damp paper towels. When the root begins to emerge, turn the bean upside down in the jar so the root is heading up. Keep the paper towels damp. Leave it for a few days. What happens?

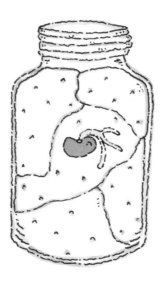

Scientists have tried growing plants out in space where there is no gravity. They found that without gravity, the plants did not know which way to grow.

4

THE WONDERS OF PLANTS

Some scientists work with plants and seeds all the time to come up with new kinds. Botanists develop new colors of roses and other flowers. They might work to

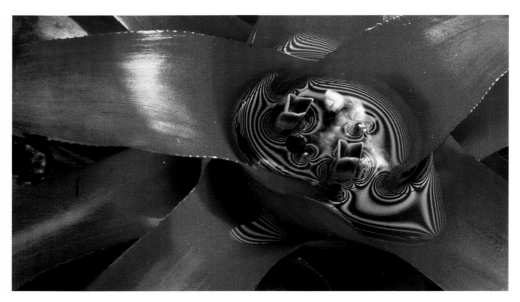

This exotic plant lives in trees in the rain forest of Brazil. It gets nutrients from water that pools in its red leaves. Insects and other organisms live in the water, too.

make better plants that can grow well with less water or in different types of soil. They might want to grow plants that resist disease or insects.

Scientists have developed bananas without seeds. They have developed chemicals that help plants to grow larger fruit or begin rooting faster.

But even without scientists, the world of plants is filled with variety. Some plants are eaten by insects, others by small animals. We eat fruits, seeds, stems, leaves, and roots. Look through your kitchen. Can you find at least one food of each of these types?

You might find apples, bananas, oranges, pears, peaches, grapes, or cherries. They are all fruits. Seeds we eat include sesame seeds, nuts, rice, oats, corn, and beans. Wheat is a seed. We grind wheat to make flour and use flour to make bread, cakes, and cookies. We eat the stem of the celery plant. We eat the leaves of lettuce, spinach, and cabbage. Roots we eat include beets and carrots.

All our food depends on sunlight, water, and soil. If we eat meat, we eat an animal that ate either plants or another animal that ate plants.

Try this:

Think about colonizing the moon. If you were in charge of designing the gardens of the colony, which plants would you include? Would you include a plot of grass to feed a cow?

How Plants Multiply

Plants make new plants in many ways. Most cannot form seeds without being *pollinated*. That means a powdery substance called pollen, usually found in flowers, passes from one plant to another.

Flowers and plants cannot move from place to place. They depend on bees and other insects to carry pollen from one flower to another. Other plants, such as oaks, aspens, and grasses, are pollinated by the wind.

The yellow powder on this bee is pollen. By carrying pollen from one flower to another, bees help flowers make seeds.

Insects are attracted to the wonderful smells and bright colors of flowers. When insects come to sip nectar from the flowers, pollen sticks to their bodies. The pollen later rubs off on another flower.

Some plants, like forsythia and strawberries, send out long, thin *runners* that travel far along the ground. New plants then grow from these runners.

Instead of pollinating, strawberry plants spread by sending out runners along the ground. These runners look like thin red stems.

You can start new plants by cutting off a piece of some plants. If you have an ivy plant, you can cut off a stem without hurting it. Then if you put the stem in water, it will grow roots and can be planted in soil.

Ask to cut a stem off a houseplant. Be sure you have a few leaves. Swedish ivy, wandering Jew, or philodendron will work well. Put the end of the stem in a glass or jar of water. Keep fresh water at the same height in the glass. After several weeks, your stem should have a number of roots. Wait about two months, then try planting the new plant in potting soil. Be gentle with those new roots as you plant them!

The Changing Seasons

What happens to plants when the weather changes? You probably have seen trees lose their leaves in the fall. When the days are shorter, trees get less sunlight. They begin to change color. This happens because the green chlorophyll breaks down and disappears when the temperature drops at night.

What happens to other plants?

The best way to observe seasonal changes in plants is to watch your own neighborhood plants. First you have to notice and remember which plants you have around you.

Try this:

Make a map of your yard or a neighborhood park.

You will want to include all the plants and animals you observe, so choose a small area. Try to identify all the plants you can. Mark them on your map.

Date your map and make notes in a notebook of what is happening with the plants. Are the leaves just emerging? Are the plants flowering? Are the leaves losing their chlorophyll?

Revisit your area every month and note the changes that occur. Be sure to date every entry. Read over your notes after several months. What changes occurred?

When you take notes on what is happening with plants, you are making *field notes*. Many scientists make extensive field notes for their projects. The more details you can observe, the more you will learn. And the more closely you watch plants, the more you will appreciate them.

Some Unusual Plants

So far, we have been working with plants that need fresh water, sunlight, and soil. They have stems, roots, leaves, and sometimes flowers. However, there are many other plants that do not.

A cactus grows where it's very dry. Instead of leaves, the cactus grows spines that keep moisture in the plant. If you spray a cactus with water, the water beads up on the surface. The surface of the plant will not let water in or out.

The Venus's-flytrap is one of the few plants that eats insects.

Some plants eat insects. The most common is the Venus's-flytrap. When an insect lands on a sensitive part of its leaf, the leaf closes. The plant traps the insect inside and digests it with the plant's own fluids.

5

WHAT WE CAN DO

You've seen that the plant kingdom has a wide variety of plants, from diatoms to sequoias, from carrots to grass. The lives of plants and animals are woven

Wildflowers in Vermont

together on this planet, making it possible for life as we know it to exist. If the balance of nature is upset, harmful things may occur.

For example, too much carbon dioxide is being produced these days by cars, factories, and utilities that burn coal or natural gas to create electricity. If there were more plants to use up the carbon dioxide, that might be all right. But the world's forests are decreasing, not increasing.

Some scientists believe too much carbon dioxide is already causing a *greenhouse effect*. Temperatures may be rising and weather patterns may be changing because of it. If it continues, oceans could rise higher and cover more land at the shores. To solve the problem, we must put the carbon dioxide–oxygen cycle back in balance.

Now that you know more about plants, maybe you will want to be a botanist and study plants. Or maybe you will want to do something about the greenhouse effect. Maybe something you discover will improve our world.

GLOSSARY

aquatic (uh-KWAH-tik)—living or growing in water

botanist (BAH-tuhn-ist)—scientist who works with plants

chlorophyll (KLORE-uh-fil)—the green-colored substance in leaves and plants

cotyledon (kah-tuh-LEED-uhn)—the part of the seed that stores food for the growing plant.

diatom (DIE-uh-tahm)—single-celled plant that lives in fresh water or seawater

erode (uh-RODE)—to wear away the earth's surface

field notes—notes scientists take when they are making observations outside, in the field

germinate (JER-min-ate)—to begin to grow or develop

greenhouse effect—the trapping of heat in the earth's atmosphere by carbon dioxide and other gases

humus (HYOO-muss)—decomposed plant or animal matter

hypothesis (hie-PAHTH-uh-sis)—a suggested explanation or answer

local plant—plant that grows naturally in nearby soil; when it's unwanted, it's usually called a weed

nutrient (NOO-tree-uhnt)—food or other substance that living things need to survive

osmosis (ahz-MOH-sis)—the movement of liquids from one cell to another

photosynthesis (foh-toh-SIN-thuh-sis)—light working on carbon dioxide, water, and chlorophyll to make new plant growth

phototropism (foh-tuh-truh-PI-zm)—growing toward light

pollinate (PAH-lin-ate)—to fertilize flowering plants with pollen

potting medium—soil or other substance in which seeds are planted in containers

reflector—surface that reflects light

runners—long, thin growths from plants, such as strawberries. They help plants spread along the ground.

sequoia (suh-KWOY-uh)—large evergreen tree of northern California

stomate (STOH-mate)—opening in a leaf that allows moisture to escape

topsoil—uppermost part of the earth; fertile soil

transpiration (tranz-puh-RAY-shun)—process by which water escapes from a plant

turgor (TER-ger) **pressure**—pressure within a plant's cells

INDEX

Italicized page numbers indicate illustrations.